Your BBQ Sauce is Best

How to Create Your Own
BBQ Sauce Recipes

by Jeff Slankard

ISBN-10: 1490496173
ISBN-13: 978-1490496177

Contents

Introduction

Never underestimate your power of creativity and imagination.

Some of the best recipes in the world come from people that are just like you. The world just doesn't know about yours yet.

You may have already played around with your creativity in the kitchen. Maybe you accidentally left out an ingredient one day, or even put too much of another ingredient.

What did you do?

You compensated. You added it later, added other additional ingredients, diluted it, masked it, or even turned it into something else.

There is never a mistake in the kitchen… just a new recipe trying to be discovered.

Think about this for a minute. You can go to a chain restaurant and get some really good food. They are consistent. You know what to expect. But then, you can go to a little hole-in-the-wall restaurant or café and get some really great food.

No… you're right… not always. I know that too. But some of the best food in the world does come from those little out-of-the-way spots.

You can make your food as good as any food… anywhere.

Don't get me wrong, though.

It's not just a matter of throwing the right combination of ingredients together and you're done. It takes using good quality fresh ingredients, bringing those flavors together in the right amounts, the right order, the right temperature, etc. Otherwise known as the process.

If you give 2 or 3 people (or even 5 or 6) the exact same recipe and ask them to go make it... you will get exactly that many different results. Even if all of them have directions to go with the list of ingredients, the results will not be the same.

But you already know this. Right?

Don't you remember how nobody could make that certain dish the way your Grandma could? Even using the identical recipe, it never turned out as good as Grandma's.

Why do you think that is?

Experience is one reason. Grandma has been doing it for a long time and has gotten pretty good. Although you being young and impressionable back then didn't hurt either.

But, her process was somehow unique and different.

Maybe Grandma used a well seasoned 40 year old cast iron skillet and no one else did. Did she sauté the garlic in butter, or toss it in later during the process... raw? Were some of the dry seasonings added during browning of the meat, or later into the liquid broth? ...and which ones? Did she use Heinz or Hunts? It could have been many things.

I once asked the owner of a restaurant why his award winning tomatillo sauce was so good. He told me that it wasn't the ingredients that made it so good... it was the process.

Actually, you know all of those people out there that have a "secret recipe" they are protecting? You know who I'm talking about... right? They might do well to protect their process and not worry so much about the recipe getting out.

So, in this book we will talk about process. We will also talk about ingredients of all types. We'll discuss some BBQ background and basics, different types of BBQ sauces used, sauce style by region of the country, plus a few recipes.

And by the way, when you see the recipes I use in this book, please note the following:

c = cup
t = teaspoon
T =Tablespoon

But remember, this process will have a lot to do with your own creativity and imagination as well. If really you want to go beyond buying a BBQ sauce in a bottle, and create something truly extraordinary, this is the way to do it.

Create your own BBQ sauce.

Before we get started, though, you should know up front that I am writing this from my own experiences. I have been cooking, BBQing, grilling, and creating original recipes for my friends and family for over 40 years. And I love it... as I'm sure you do too.

So let's get started

Your BBQ Sauce is Best

1
What Is BBQ

What's The Big Mystery?

There is just something about the smell that relaxes me.

And you know how smells can trigger memories?

Every time I smell it, I am taken back to a whole lifetime of good memories. All of them are of leisure and relaxation. But you know that! You love it, too. I guess we're just lucky.

Not everybody has that.

Is it BBQ, barbecue, barbeque, or Bar-B-Q?

Pick one and use whichever you like. They all refer to the same thing. When you see a sign advertising a place to eat, you know what it means. It doesn't really matter how they spell it.

The real question about BBQ is not how it is spelled, but what is it? There may be disagreement about this for generations.

BBQ has been around since colonial times (probably longer). Confusion and disagreement still exist today.

I really think BBQ came about through a combination of influences (Caribbean, African, Europe, American Indians, cowboys, etc.). People don't agree on its origin, so they can't agree on a definition.

The purists will tell you that BBQ is slow smoking with indirect heat from a hardwood fire. Some will say it must be pork. Others insist that you must use a sauce. People in general will also refer to grilling as BBQ (that really ruffles the feathers).

The details can get very specific. Type of fuel, cooking temperature, whether to use a rub, sauce or marinade, and, yes... whether to use aluminum foil or not, are just a few possible variations.

And naturally, not everyone agrees on the details.

There are so many variations to BBQ that it can't really be given just one definition that is acceptable to everybody. I try not to get bogged down with the details. It's kind of like politics, depending on who you talk to, you can't win an argument.

Speaking of definitions (and I was), Webster's dictionary defines barbecue as:

1. to roast or broil on a rack or revolving spit over or before a source of heat such as hot coals

2. to cook in a highly seasoned vinegar sauce

3. framework for supporting meat over a fire

4. a large animal (as a steer) roasted whole or split over an open fire or a fire pit

5. a social gathering especially in the open air at which barbecued food is eaten

6. an often portable fireplace over which meat and fish are roasted

So it looks like BBQ is ...
what gets cooked
how you cook it
what you cook it with
and **where** it's cooked.

You can see why people can't agree?

What do you mean, you're confused? You still don't know what BBQ is? Well, I guess there is only one way to clear this up.

Just accept my invitation and come to my barbecue, and I'll show you how to barbeque some BBQ on my Bar-B-Q.

Smoking

How the food is cooked has a lot to do with the equipment used. True BBQ is considered by many to be cooked slowly using indirect heat at temperatures between 200 to 240 degrees with a hardwood fire.

There are many variations of this type of cooking, too.

The equipment varies in size and design. The heat varies based on equipment and the pit master. The heat source varies such as hickory, mesquite, oak, etc. There are different forms of fuel such as cut wood, chunk coal, charcoal briquettes, etc.

Grilling

Grilling is the very popular form of outdoor cooking that uses direct heat. It's done at a higher temperature and used for cooking smaller pieces. It is much quicker than smoking and has as many, if not more, variations in technique.

All of the different cooking techniques have their own set of pros and cons. Most people have a preferred method, although some dabble in all of it. The real die hards become experts in their chosen techniques.

We didn't even get into the gathering (restaurant, back yard, catered, competitions, parties, etc.). That's alright. We'll save that discussion for another time, another day and another book. Remind me about it later.

Out there in cyberspace, there are some excellent websites that go into great detail about cooking methods and techniques. For the purpose of this book we are just laying a basic foundation of BBQ because we want to discuss sauces in more detail.

I'd better point out something else about my use of the term, too. You'll find that I almost always use "BBQ".

That's just because it's quicker and easier to write.

When in the company of the average Joe, I know what he means when he says BBQ. But, on the other hand, I also know how strict the definition can be in the company of others. So, associate with your own kind, if you must.

But, let's all get along...OK?

Since barbecue is (according to Webster) the what, how, with what, where and when of cooking, I will use it that way too.

Therefore, I will use the term BBQ to include not only smoking, but direct heat grilling, cooking with sauce, no sauce, marinades, rubs, or any other form of outdoor cooking for that matter.

It's all good.

2
Why Use Marinade Recipes?
Give Me 5 Good Reasons

1. Flavor

Probably the number one reason to use marinade recipes is for the flavor. Your freedom to choose ingredients that suit your taste, makes it easy (see reason number 3) to customize the flavor.

The flavor comes from all of the ingredients and can vary greatly. But, the choices of herbs, seasonings and spices are limitless when you consider the possible combinations.

2. Tenderization

Marinade recipes do not actually tenderize the meat. But, the acid in the marinade will chemically alter the muscle fibers, giving it that effect. Since acids can be vinegar, wine, beer, lemon juice, lime juice, etc., they also have a great influence on the flavor (see reason number 1).

This tenderization effect can also be caused by enzymes found in some foods. These enzymes are in foods such as raw onion, fresh ginger, pineapple, and green papaya. The enzymes denature (or break down) muscle fibers similar to the way acids do.

Another even more powerful form of "tenderization" comes from fermented milk products like yogurt and buttermilk. It is the bacteria in them, with their digestive qualities, that acts upon the meat to denature it. Meat seems to stay moister when these are used.

3. It's Simple

Marinade recipes are simple in that they only contain an acid, oil, and seasonings. OK... maybe some recipes can get pretty long with all of their ingredients (seasonings, spices and such). Some people do tend to go overboard (like some BBQ rub recipes).

But, it is still very straightforward. Here is an example of a basic marinade recipe:

1/2 c olive oil
1/4 c lime juice
1/4 c Tequila
1 packet of Italian salad dressing

Blend all of the ingredients together and add the meat. Use a glass or non-aluminum bowl to prevent discoloration. All surfaces of the meat must come in contact with the marinade. So, turn the meat every 30 minutes or so.

You might, however, rather use a zipped plastic bag. This will allow all surfaces of the meat to be in contact with the marinade at the same time. You will probably use less marinade, too.

Marinating times vary from a few minutes, to 24 hours. A combination of factors is figured into how long something should be marinated. Type of meat, size of the meat, delicateness, strength of the acid, and temperature are some things to consider.

Small pieces of fish in lime juice at room temperature would only need a few minutes to marinate. A 10 pound beef brisket in soy sauce in the refrigerator might need to marinate overnight or longer.

4. Good for You

When meat is flame cooked at high temperature, cancer-causing agents called Heterocyclic Amines (HCAs) can be produced. You may have seen it in the news at different times over the last few years. The use of marinades may actually discourage the formation of HCAs on char-grilled meats.

Of course you still have to be careful and follow some basic food safety practices when using marinade recipes, too. Clean surfaces thoroughly and avoid excess contamination. Throw out any leftover marinade that has come into contact with raw meat. And always marinate in the refrigerator.

5. It's Been Done for Centuries

In ancient times people tried different ways to preserve meat. If you remember from History class, refrigerators didn't work back then (no place to plug them in).

They tried salt, sun and other ways of drying the meat. They tried oils, and maybe even accidentally, acids of different types. People started using spices, (probably also accidentally), to improve the flavor. Worcestershire sauce is one of the results of those early attempts to preserve foods.

Today, marinade recipes are fairly standard (acid, oil, seasonings). But that's far from saying "they're all alike". You have the power to make them taste the way you want. Delete, add, or adjust ingredients to suit your own taste. You will get better with practice (you really will). Take the benefit of all those centuries of experimentation and try it.

3
More on Marinades

When it comes to BBQ, marinade recipes get used a lot. Marinades are sauces that flavor meat. Sometimes, though, they are dry rubs. They are a little different than BBQ sauces (which also flavor meat).

A marinade is used before cooking; BBQ sauce is used during and/or after cooking.

The ingredients of the marinade (which, by the way, are an acid, an oil, and seasonings) get mixed together. Then the meat (or vegetable) sits in it for a while to take on those flavors. The whole idea is to add flavor.

Originally, using marinades was a form of preserving food. The acid in the marinade recipe chemically alters the muscle fibers of the meat. It doesn't technically tenderize it, but it does soften the outer layer of the meat.

Ingredients in Marinade Recipes

Acids
Acids used in marinade recipes can be:
Vinegar
Bourbon
Wine
Beer

Lemon juice
Lime juice
Other fruit juice

And that is not all of them. Combinations like tequila and lime go together very well (do Margaritas come to mind?). Although these acids "chemically alter the muscle fibers", they also provide tremendous flavor, as well as the tenderizing effect.

Vinegar is probably the most commonly used acid in marinades (and salad dressings too, come to think of it). I prefer using apple cider vinegar.

Enzymes found in pineapple, green papaya, fresh ginger and raw onion can denature (break down) muscle fibers like the acids do. Yogurt and buttermilk are actually more powerful than any of them. But, they soften the meat in a little different way.

These fermented milk products use the digestive qualities of the bacteria found in them. Meats seem to stay moister when cooked with these.

The acids tend to cook the meat in a way very similar to heat. Because of this, marinating should be limited. The time varies based on how long that chemical change takes.

The stronger the acid, or the more delicate the meat, the shorter the time should be. (More on this later)

Oils

Oil is used in marinade recipes to maintain moisture. It acts as a thickener and helps distribute the other seasonings. If you look at a bottle of vinaigrette salad dressing, you're actually looking at a marinade (vinegar, oil, and seasonings).

Shake it up... see how the oil keeps the seasonings suspended. After a while, though, it separates again into layers.

Oils can also change the flavor of your dishes. Think about using sesame oil, peanut oil, olive oil, fire oil, and others.

Seasonings for Marinade Recipes

Here is where you have total control.

The combination of what you use here controls the final flavor. Not only the combination, but the amounts of each as well as when and how you combine them.

Some common ingredients found in marinade recipes include seasonings like:

garlic
onion
ginger
soy sauce
Worcestershire sauce
Tabasco
salt
pepper
chili powder
oregano

Not all necessarily in the same marinade. But the list of choices could be huge. Literally thousands of choices and combinations are possible.

As you know, different cuisines of the world have their own groups of seasonings. Marinade recipes can take advantage of this to create the right flavors for a specific theme. For example, soy, sesame oil, ginger, and garlic could serve as a base for an oriental marinade.

Recently a proud restaurant owner (Ernesto) from San Antonio was telling me about his award winning tomatillo sauce. He told me, "it's not the ingredients (that makes it good), **it's the process**".

Give two different people the same recipe with the same ingredients list, and ask them to go into separate kitchens to make it. Do you think they will turn out the same result?

Probably not. Unless maybe the recipe was very specific about not only how much to use, but in what form, in what order, in what manner, etc.

For instance, garlic powder or fresh garlic... whole, sliced or minced... tomato juice or stewed tomatoes... dried cilantro or fresh... jalapeño or Serrano... fresh or roasted... seeded or not... heated or refrigerated... stirred or pureed... strained or not... are you getting the idea?

Can you see that you are in the driver's seat on this trip?

This is where the fun comes into the picture. Be creative. Try new things. Not just substitute dried cilantro with fresh cilantro, but splash it with fresh lime juice as well.

Here is one of the best things about doing all this. The next time, you will know much more than you did before. And your confidence level will really begin to climb. You're just one notch closer to being that local expert.

Take your time and enjoy.

Chances are that you won't make a masterpiece on the first try. No biggie. You will need to taste along the way. After all, that's what you are going for is that perfect flavor.

You will probably have an idea of what you want. Maybe it's extra sweetness. Maybe it's a little more fire or tang.

Whatever it is, work toward it in your marinade recipes. Many ingredients are very potent, such as liquid smoke or Worcestershire sauce. Too much is hard to overcome.

Bringing it all Together

When getting the marinade recipes ready for use, they should be emulsified. The acid, which is mostly water, and the oil won't mix. So, when it is blended together, it's not a solution (like saltwater). It's not a mixture (like milk and flour).

It's an emulsion, because it is temporary and will separate (like the salad dressing).

Here is a way to bring this oil and acid together. Wisk the acid while adding the oil a little bit at a time. By adding the oil slowly, it is broken down into tiny droplets that will stay suspended (for a few hours anyway).

Either do that, or put it all into a sealable jar and shake it like crazy for a minute or so.

When creating your marinade recipe, you will need to use a container or tumbler that is non-reactive (non-aluminum). Otherwise you may get discolored meats.

I like to use glass. Many people use zipped plastic bags. They work very well. Just make sure they are sealed properly. They allow you to use a smaller amount of marinade and get better coverage.

All parts of the meat need to come in contact with the marinade. So, depending on what you use, you will need to turn the meat every 30 minutes or hour.

A Little Bit About Safety

Remember, this is raw meat that you are dealing with. Once it comes into contact with the marinade, it is contaminated. Be clean.

Any area of spilled marinade should be cleaned and disinfected as if it was touched by raw meat. For the same reason, leftover marinade should be thrown out and never reused.

Let's say... for some reason you seemed to think that this original recipe of yours was too good to waste. And let's say... you wanted to use it as a basting sauce. Well, if it's that good, I can see your point.

If that's what you want to do, you will need to boil the marinade for several minutes to kill any remaining bacteria. If you want to use some of it as a dipping sauce, simply reserve some of it before you use it as the marinade.

Flame cooking at high temperatures can produce cancer-causing agents called Heterocyclic Amines (HCAs). Marinades may discourage formation of HCAs in char-grilled meats. (Just thought you might want to know.)

Always marinate in the refrigerator (unless it will be for 30 minutes or less). The same theory applies (food safety). Keep the bacteria from forming.

Sure flavors will be absorbed quicker at a higher temperature, but why risk salmonella for a little difference in time? Besides, we've got time. Right?

What about the time?

Through my research of marinades, I have found marinating times as long as several days. Evidently no standard rules apply.

If something is marinated too long, it will become mushy and discolored. You can tell from looking. Meat will begin to turn gray, chicken and pork will start to look white, and fish will turn opaque.

If this starts to happen, take it out of the marinade. Dry it off, wrap it in plastic, and put it back into the refrigerator until you are ready to cook it.

It's like seasoning with salt. Just a little bit doesn't change the taste much. A little more may be just right. But, too much can ruin it.

The best I can do is to give you some guidelines. I (personal opinion here) would not marinate anything over 24 hours (even beef). Usually overnight is plenty. And back off even more than that if you have small cuts, tender cuts, or a high acid marinade recipe.

For chicken and pork, I marinate from 2 to 6 hours. I would say overnight would be the maximum. Fish, though, is more delicate. Between 20 minutes and 2 hours is usually enough. Vegetables... the same as fish.

I have talked to butchers that tell me marinating times for a good quality steak should be 15 minutes or less. They say that it covers up the flavor of the meat if left too long.

Some people even say steaks are better without a marinade at all. Isn't that the way it ought to be, though?

Everyone fixing good food to suit their own taste.

If you like marinades, use them. If you don't like them,

don't use them. It's all up to you and your taste.

Take these times as a guide and adjust them as needed. Times are a part of your marinade recipes. Adjust them as you would the ingredients. Try to get that right balance of flavor and tenderness.

4
BBQ Mop Recipes
Say Goodbye to Dry Meat

BBQ mop recipes are used by true BBQ fans, as well as professional on the competition circuit. If you are one of those fans, you know what I mean. You take every step you can to improve your BBQ.

A good mop is one of those steps.

A mop is a thin basting sauce used during cooking (usually during slow smoking). It adds a little flavor, but primarily, it's used to keep the meat from getting dry.

They call it a mop because it is applied with a mop (or something smaller that looks like a mop). Although some people use a spray bottle instead of a brush or mop.

To apply a mop during smoking means that you have to open the door (or lid). When that happens, heat and smoke escape. This causes the temperature around the meat to drop. (And after all that work you did to get the temperature just right, and keep it that way.)

So, we have uncovered a new art form, when it comes to BBQ. This art is the balancing act of maintaining moisture (with BBQ mop recipes) and maintaining a constant temperature (around 220 degrees).

If you apply a mop too often, the temperature drops, meat cooks unevenly, and it takes longer to cook. The longer the meat smokes (without a mop), the drier it will become.

Usually a mop is applied every hour, or at least 2 or 3 times during cooking. At most apply it every 30 minutes. When you do apply it, be quick about it and get the lid closed again.

Stay Away from the Sugar

Mops must not be too high in sugar content or they will burn during cooking. Sugars, tomato sauce and ketchup will all burn.

Mops may have these ingredients in them, as well as other things like brown sugar, butter, oils, and BBQ sauce. But their amounts are usually small.

If they were too high, like in BBQ sauce, burning would be the final crust.

One of the most common and simple BBQ mop recipes is this:

90% apple juice
10% oil

This is thin enough it can also be applied using a spray bottle. Other mops may have additional seasonings to help with flavor. But they all are generally thin.

Beer and beef stock are commonly used as a base in mops, too. These are some ingredients in the "Texas" style of a mop.

2 cans of beer
8 oz Worcestershire sauce
1 chopped white onion
1 sliced lemon

Additional/Optional ingredients
1 cup of black coffee (brewed)
several cloves of chopped garlic

a few chopped jalapeño peppers
a little butter
6 oz yellow mustard
4 oz flavored vinegar (such as cider)
hot pepper sauce or flakes
honey or BBQ sauce (if you need a little sweetness)

Heat this up and keep it warm on your firebox during cooking. If you start to run a little low, just add another can of beer. By the way... only one can of beer is needed for the recipe. Drink the other one while you are making it.

Some of the best BBQ pit masters in the world swear by their BBQ mop recipes. It can greatly affect the outcome of your meat. Experiment, have fun, get another drink, and try again.

5
BBQ Rub Recipe
The Other Marinade

A BBQ rub recipe goes hand in hand with a good mop sauce. Together, they are the key to good slow smoking.

Dry rubs are used to coat the surface of the meat. They create a great tasting crust. Some rubs, such as jerk, can be in the form of a paste. They serve the same purpose, though... flavor.

Many times rubs are used as marinades. They can be left on the meat from a few minutes to 24 hours before cooking. Again, their purpose is to flavor, not to tenderize, as with a marinade.

One of the important things to remember is that there needs to be enough salt in the rub. Salt will cause moisture to be drawn out of the surface of the meat.

Another thing to keep in mind is that the amount of sugar should not be too high. Too much sugar will cause burning, not to mention a bad taste.

Slight Disagreement

Some folks say not to use salt or sugar at all in rubs. Well, I can see their point. Salt does draw moisture. And sugar does burn.

But, I always use both. Not just to be contrary, but because each one adds tremendous flavor dimension. And, if you don't go overboard with either one, and find a good proportion, you get much better tasting meat than without them.

Keeping the temperature at 225 degrees isn't that hard to do. That's where it needs to be anyway, with or without sugar. And what little moisture is drawn from the meat by the salt, gets absorbed by the rub and helps the seasoning flavor the meat even better.

A BBQ rub is like a BBQ sauce. They are both available, ready-made, commercially. There are recipes available in books and online. They can both be easily made to match your own unique tastes.

Many of the seasonings used in a BBQ sauce can also be used in a BBQ rub recipe. Remember... you can always take the easy way out and just buy a ready-made rub at the store.

But, that would take the fun out of it, wouldn't it?

When you get it right, you will guard your own BBQ rub recipe the way the pros do.

The right proportion of salt and sugar will make your rub a good one. This proportion will change too, with different cooking times and styles of cooking. If you want to grill food and use a rub (nothing wrong with that), then don't use any sugar at all.

It will burn... remember? Always avoid that.

You will be able to use more sugar when you slow smoke, because it is done with indirect heat. And the temperatures are lower than grilling. I wouldn't let the temperature get above 225 degrees, though.

The combination of salt and sugar will affect the taste, but also the amount of moisture, caramelization, and (of course) burning.

Some of the other ingredients may have some sweetness in them. They are all in it for the flavor, though. They won't really affect the sugar content of the BBQ rub recipe.

Ready, Set, Rub

When you are ready to apply the rub, start by coating all surfaces of the meat with Worcestershire sauce (my favorite). If you don't like Worcestershire sauce, use another liquid like an oil.

Rubbing the meat with liquid will assure that all of your dry seasonings stick and stay there. This may turn into more of a paste, but... that's OK, isn't it? Remember if you don't like an ingredient, don't use it in your BBQ rub recipe.

Now, I'm not trying to give you orders, just making suggestions. If you prefer not to use a liquid, that's OK, too. Some of your rub may fall off and be left behind, that's all.

If you are going to grill, you may want the rub to sit on the meat for a while so you get some extra flavor transfer. But, if you've got a big brisket that you're going to smoke for 10 or 12 hours, get after it.

Your Kick-Start

These ingredients can make you a very nice rub.

salt
brown sugar
cumin
chili powder
black pepper
cayenne pepper
paprika

Use the same measure of each ingredient. Make them all 1 tsp, 1Tbs, or 1/4 cup, your choice. It's just a matter of how much you want to make or how much meat you need to rub.

Since you haven't tried it yet, just make a small batch. You will probably want to adjust it for your taste anyway.

You may want a little more paprika and a little less cayenne. You may want a little extra chili powder, like we do in Texas. You may even want to trade out dry mustard for the cumin.

I don't know what you like, but you do. Make it into your signature BBQ rub recipe.

Here is another one to get you thinking.

1/4 c brown sugar
1/4 c vinegar
1/8 c salt
1/8 c onion powder
1/8 c paprika
1 Tbs black pepper
1 Tbs chili powder
1 Tbs dry mustard
1 tsp thyme
1 tsp ginger

Notice this recipe has vinegar in it. Since it is a wet rub, you won't need to put Worcestershire sauce on the meat first. You are better off in this case to pat the meat dry before applying the wet rub.

Naturally, this is here for you to manipulate any way you want. Add additional ingredients like garlic powder, tarragon, allspice, etc. Or maybe make changes like dry mustard for cumin, or whatever floats your boat.

Please enjoy this as you experiment. If it's no fun, find something that is. Zero in on something you are passionate about, and enjoy the ride. For all of you enjoyable fans of BBQ out there... get another drink, and let's try again.

6
BBQ Sauce

So far, all we have discussed has been different forms of BBQ sauce. Mops, marinades, and even dry rubs are all sauces that use similar ingredients to flavor the meat (or chicken, or fish, or veggies, etc.).

These are all sauces that you can create in the exact same way you would create any BBQ sauce. BBQ sauce is usually thought of as a finishing sauce or a dipping sauce, but don't discount the importance of mops, marinades and rubs.

Part of the reason for this discussion was to show how the ingredients work together. The other reason is to get you thinking about your control over these recipes, and how they can be manipulated.

Now it's time to jump into how you can create your own BBQ sauce.

Start with the Basics;

2 cup ketchup
1-1/2 cup brown sugar
1/3 cup vinegar
2 tablespoon Worcestershire sauce
1 teaspoon salt

Add a little of the following;

1/2 can of Beer
1 tablespoon Whiskey
Cider Vinegar
Anchovy Paste
Anise Spice
Apple Juice
Bay Leaves
Celery Salt
Chili Powder
Chinese Five Spice
Coconut Milk
Corn Starch, for thickening
Corn Syrup
Cumin Powder
Dijon Mustard or Mustard Powder
Enchilada Sauce
Garlic Cloves or Garlic Powder
Hoisin Sauce (Peking Sauce)
Honey
Hot Peppers, minced
Hot Sauce, Cayenne or Black Pepper
Instant Coffee Powder
Apple, Orange, Pineapple, Lemon or Lime juice
Liquid smoke
Maple Syrup
Molasses
Onion Powder or Minced Onions
Oyster Sauce
Paprika
Peanut Butter
Salsa
7 Up, Cola or other soda
Soy sauce
Tomato Juice
Tomato Sauce

And there you have it.

Well, not quite, but that's close.

All you really need to do, though, is just get started. Instead of starting with a list of ingredients like I gave you (sorry), start with a recipe.

Let the experience of those before you get you onto the right track. Use a recipe. Start with someone else's. They know what they are doing.

Your creativity and imagination can take over from there. You don't have to go through all of the hard work that it took for BBQ to become what it is today. Work with what's available... all of those recipes that are already out there.

It all really comes down to this:

Start with an existing recipe
and
Tweak it.

(Adjust it by changing, adding or deleting ingredients or the process)

I know that is a very simplified way to put it, but that's it, except for your creativity and imagination. You supply the tweaking. Your combined experience, confidence, knowledge, creativity and imagination will do the tweaking.

Don't sell yourself short. You can do this as well as anyone. You are already increasing your knowledge by reading this book. You will be gaining experience and confidence the first time you tweak a recipe.

You have tremendous control over how these recipes turn out. You have the power to create something truly remarkable. I wish I could tell you

"add another 1/2 tsp of salt" or,
"add a tsp of pickle juice" or,
"toast the sesame seeds before you add them".

But even if I could do that, it would take away from being **your** recipe. When you make decisions like that, it strengthens the fact that it is absolutely your recipe.

Continue to have fun by practicing, continually learning and getting better at making those kinds of small but important decisions. You **will** get better at it.

It's all a matter of taste.

What will guide you, as you adjust (tweak) a recipe, is your own personal taste. That's what tells you that something needs to be sweeter, or needs more spice, more salt, etc.

Besides the main base ingredients, the herbs, spices, and seasonings are your tools to make great BBQ sauce. Generally speaking fresh is always better. But there are always a few spices out there that will only be available in dry or powdered form.

Do some experimenting on your own too. As an example take something in isolation, like **salt**.

Salt is a powerful seasoning.

It has been used for centuries to preserve food. It draws moisture. It is commonly used in all types of cooking as a flavor enhancer. It keeps food from being bland. You know… salt. You use it too… right?

Take this little test…

and checkout for yourself just how powerful it is as a flavor enhancer. Take a fresh slice of peach and taste it. Take the time to really taste it. Close your eyes and concentrate on the flavor.

Good! Right?

Now add a small amount of salt and take another bite. Close your eyes again and concentrate on the flavor.

Good! Huh? Maybe even a little better?

You can tell that salt can really improve flavor, can't you? The secret about using salt, though, is this

if you can taste it… you've used too much.

Add seasoning to improve the taste, without leaving the hint of how you did it. There is the art we should all strive to master.

That's why it is so important to taste after using salt (or any other seasoning, for that matter).

Add small amounts at a time.

Taste until you get the flavor you want.

You can add a little more if you need to, but you can't take it out if you have too much. The only way out of that is to add more of everything else. And that's not always possible.

7
Best BBQ Sauce Recipe?
No Such Thing

Picking out the best BBQ sauce recipe is like trying to decide which of your children you love the most. It's just not that cut and dried (simple).

If you are looking for the best BBQ sauce, you will find it wherever you go.

In other words, if you go to Memphis and ask what is the best BBQ sauce, most of the people there will tell you a Memphis style sauce.

It's like Clint Black's song says, "wherever you go, there you are".

Without getting into all the history and background, let's just say that BBQ sauce varies by region of the country. If anything is agreed upon in the world of BBQ, it's that BBQ sauce is different depending on where you go.

If I were to tell you the best BBQ sauce, it would be based entirely on opinion. Chances are that we wouldn't agree about it, either. There are far too many sauces that please so many people to pick one as the best.

Actually the **best BBQ sauce is your favorite**.

So, you now must decide for yourself which recipe is the best. Because... no one else knows what you like, better than you do. Most people have their own choice of what's the best

BBQ sauce, but nobody can agree.

There are just too many. Even in areas within the sub-regions of regions have their own variations of the same style (what a mouthful).

Who cares which sauce is the best? You do... right? (Say right) OK, then....we know the best BBQ sauce recipe is the one that is your favorite. The best way to find that out is to make it yourself.

So, here we go.

BBQ sauces have combinations of sweet, sour, spicy, and tangy ingredients. The primary ingredients for most styles of sauce are tomato (sauce, paste, or ketchup), vinegar, spices and sweetness, or combinations of these.

The Memphis style of BBQ sauce is a good place to start, since it has a moderate balance of sweet, sour, spicy, and tang. Here is a basic...

Memphis style BBQ sauce

4 Tbs butter
1/4 c chopped onion
1 c tomato sauce
1 c vinegar
1/4 c Worcestershire sauce
1 Tbs brown sugar
1 tsp salt
1/2 tsp black pepper
1/8 tsp cayenne pepper
Dash Tabasco sauce

Sauté the onion in butter, then add the remaining ingredients. Heat the mixture until it thickens (15 to 20 minutes).

Any of the ingredients can be changed, added or deleted. A BBQ sauce can be as simple as tomato sauce and Worcestershire, or even vinegar and pepper flakes. But you can also make it as complex as you like, too. You could even use salsa as a base ingredient.

Notice, in the above recipe, that tomato sauce and vinegar are of equal amounts. These are the two prime ingredients that will determine a basic style. As the ratio of these ingredients change, so does the location of where it is made.

Kansas City style sauce is thick, sticky and sweet. To change the above recipe to a KC style, try reducing the vinegar to 1/4 cup and replace the Worcestershire with dark molasses. Add a few select seasonings like paprika, chili powder, and allspice (maybe a touch of cinnamon).

To go the other direction from Memphis, change the tomato sauce to 1/2 cup of ketchup and add some garlic, cloves and 1 cup of water. Increase the brown sugar to 1/2 cup. This will result in a thinner BBQ sauce similar to that used in North Carolina.

A Texas style sauce would mean to decrease the vinegar to 1/2 cup and add 1 1/2 cups of water. Add some additional celery, garlic, paprika, and (of course) chili powder.

This may sound like a lot of work, but it is also a lot of fun, too. It's really, though, the best way for you to answer that question, "what is the best BBQ sauce recipe?".

And you don't have to start with this recipe, either. There are many, many, many of them available in cookbooks and online. Find one that is close to what you want (thick, thin, sweet, spice, etc.), get yourself another drink, and let yourself go.

There may be no such thing as the best, but this is a way you can find your favorite. And by the way, you will know it when you find it.

8
BBQ Sauce Recipes with Style

BBQ sauce recipes have as many styles as there are BBQ. Some are thick and some are thin and watery. Some are sweet, some are sour, and some are hot and spicy. What a better choice for your own special recipe than a BBQ sauce.

BBQ sauces usually flavor meats at the end of the cooking process. Most of them usually have sugar, which can burn. That is why BBQ sauce recipes call for you to put it on during the last 30 minutes or less of cooking time. These sweet sauces are also used as a dipping sauce.

Styles of the Big Guys

Different regions of the country have their own style of BBQ sauce. There are five major styles. They are as follows:

Carolina
thin
vinegar based
not too spicy
not too sweet

Memphis
thin

tomato and vinegar based
not too spicy
not too sweet

St. Louis
medium
tomato and vinegar based
spicy
sweet

Kansas City
thick
tomato based
not too spicy
sweet

Texas
medium to thin
tomato based
spicy
not too sweet

OK. OK. I know there is more than that.

But these are in the big league. They are the most well known. There are many other small sub-groups around the country (not to mention the world). There are a slew of them in the state of Georgia alone. But, we can't mention them all, can we?.

The vinegar based barbecue sauces are the thinner ones (like Carolina and Memphis style). They are used more often during cooking because they are less likely to burn.

A mop sauce is one that is used as a basting sauce applied with a brush or mop during cooking. Mops are very thin and mostly based on vinegar or fruit juices.

Thicker sauces (like Kansas City style) are usually sweeter and generally applied after cooking to avoid burning. Texas style is tomato based and usually spicy.

St. Louis style hits the middle. It's not thick or thin, is both vinegar and tomato based, and both sweet and spicy. But I've got to tell you... there are more varieties of a barbecue sauce recipe than you can shake a stick at (lots).

Ingredients

Ingredients for BBQ sauce recipes are not as simple as the acid, oil, and seasonings of a marinade. They will definitely have seasonings; but they may or may not have an acid or oil.

The most common styles of BBQ sauce have vinegar, tomato sauce, ketchup, mustard, or combinations as a base. Some of these following ingredients are common if not standard in some BBQ sauce recipes. Feel free to add whatever you like, or whatever you think might give it a good or unique flavor.

molasses
chili peppers (of all types)
cayenne
paprika
brown sugar
honey
Worcestershire
garlic
onion
ginger
soy sauce
cumin
cilantro
thyme

Well, you get the idea (and this is only a few).
Spices come from all parts of the globe. So this list could go on... and on... and on...

Jeff Slankard

A Basic BBQ Sauce Recipe

Here is a basic recipe for BBQ sauce for you to consider.

1/4 c cider vinegar
1/2 c ketchup
1/2 c water
3 Tbs brown sugar
1 tsp chili powder
1 tsp salt
1/2 tsp black peper

Combine all ingredients
Mix well
Refrigerate until use
It can't get any simpler than that.

The vinegar/ketchup base can vary greatly from one recipe to the next. Those base ingredients could have a different ratio. The amounts could be increased or decreased, or be something completely different (like tomato sauce).

Changing any of the other flavorings and seasonings is entirely up to you, your taste, and your imagination.

With some recipes for BBQ sauce you will simply mix up the ingredients and use it immediately (as above). Others will require you to heat it first.

Be aware that using something like ketchup (catsup) will give you a different flavor depending on which brand you use. Heinz (my favorite) tastes different than Hunt's or other brands.

Let's say this is not your style. If this doesn't suit your taste, go a different direction.

For instance, you may want a more sweet KC style of sauce. OK. Start small. Begin with

1 c tomato sauce (or ketchup if you prefer)
1/2 c molasses
1 tsp chili powder

1 tsp paprika
1 tsp onion powder
1 tsp garlic powder
1/2 tsp allspice
1/2 tsp cinnamon
1/2 tsp pepper

Heat this while you are combining ingredients. The molasses will thin down and make it easier. If it is too thick add a little vinegar to thin it as needed.

If you like, you could add a touch of hot sauce, curry powder, or liquid smoke. It's your sauce, you know. Make it like you want.

I suppose you have noticed that I use brown sugar and molasses quite often in my ingredients. With the added sugar be aware that it will burn if on the grill too long. So most BBQ sauces, like this one, are usually applied during the last few minutes of cooking.

I do know that many people must have a sugar free BBQ sauce to be able to enjoy it. I am just used to using what I like. However, there are ways to create delicious sugar free versions of your favorite BBQ sauce recipes.

Go Forth and Create

As you make changes, taste along the way. If you make major changes to a recipe, do it in small batches and take notes. If you hit on a good one (like another K.C. Masterpiece), be able to duplicate it (and sell it if it's really good).

When it comes to BBQ sauce recipes, there really are no rules or limitations.

Feel free to sauté onions and garlic before adding liquids.

Toast your seasonings before use.

Roast peppers if you would like.

Simmer the sauce for a while.

Strain it or even puree it if you prefer.

Just make a batch and have fun.

Good luck to you. And don't worry about the imperfect ones. Those give us valuable experience and reinforce why we start with small batches. The more you do, the better you get.

9
Kansas City BBQ Sauce

If you like it thick and sweet, Kansas City BBQ sauce is the style for you. Most of the time it is so sweet that it's sticky. Maybe that's why it's so good.

Here is a Kansas City BBQ sauce recipe for you to try and then tweak (that's modify and adjust for you non-geek type).

2 Tbl vegetable oil
2 Tbl butter
1 onion (chopped)
2 cloves garlic (minced)
1 bottle ketchup (16 oz)
1/2 c molasses
1/2 c dark brown sugar
4 Tbl Worcestershire sauce
1/4 c mustard
1/4 c lemon juice
2 Tbl cider vinegar
2 tsp hot sauce
1/2 tsp salt

Place the oil and butter in a large cast iron pot over medium-low heat. Sauté onion and garlic until soft (not browned). Add the remaining ingredients and stir. Continue to simmer slowly, stirring frequently, for an additional 30 minutes.

Make It Yours

Please realize that with any style of sauce there is a great deal of variation within the style. It's no different with the Kansas City style of BBQ sauce. This recipe fits the style, but has plenty of room for customizing.

If this turns out too thick for you, simply add a little water, vinegar, beer, or root beer. If, by chance, you need a little extra sweetness, try adding some dark corn syrup or honey.

Or maybe you would like a little more spice. Think about adding some chili powder, cayenne pepper, or sage. Many forms of Kansas City BBQ sauce also have allspice and/or mace.

Don't feel like you have to make additions or deletions to this recipe, though. You can still make it unique by simply adding more or less of an existing ingredient.

You may want 4 cloves of garlic or maybe just one. Adjust any of them that you want. I would suggest changing only one thing at a time, though, so you know the result.

The extra sweetness in this style of BBQ sauce is great with ribs. But, however you decide to use this version of KC BBQ sauce, be careful about using it on the grill.

Only apply the sauce during the last 15 or 20 minutes of cooking time. It will burn easily because of the high sugar content.

10
Texas BBQ Sauce Recipe

A Texas BBQ sauce recipe must first fit the style to be considered a Texas BBQ recipe. It must have a fairly equal split of ketchup and vinegar. This makes it thinner than a Kansas City style, but thicker than a North Carolina style.

It must also have a little more spice than sweetness. This will make it spicier than Kansas City style and not as sweet. Just remember that the following recipe is in a particular style (Texas), and is not necessarily **the** Texas BBQ sauce recipe.

In the Texas Style

There are many variations of this one style of sauce. So this is one of many Texas BBQ sauce recipes that are possible.

1 medium onion, chopped
3 cloves garlic, minced
1 C Ketchup
1 C Apple Cider Vinegar
1/4 C Worcestershire Sauce
1/4 C brown sugar
2 Tbl prepared mustard
2 Tbl chili powder

2 tsp cumin seed, crushed
1 tsp celery seed, crushed
1 tsp black pepper
1/2 tsp salt
2 strips Bacon, chopped

In a cast iron pot over medium heat, cook the bacon until crisp. Remove bacon and add onion and garlic. Sauté for several minutes, then add chili powder and cook an additional minute.

Add the remaining ingredients and simmer for 15 to 30 minutes. Bacon pieces may be added back to the sauce, if desired. If the sauce is too thick, additional vinegar, apple cider, or water may be added.

This recipe will make any BBQ a Texas BBQ. Recipes of this style still have a lot of room for customization. Just try to keep the general balance of sweet and spice as well as the ketchup to vinegar ratio.

A Texas BBQ sauce recipe must have those balances. Otherwise it begins to look more like a different style.

Time to Get Creative Again

Never forget that any recipe (no matter who wrote it or where it came from) is what someone came up with through experimentation. They did it specifically that way because they liked the taste.

You may not like it. So turn it into something that you do like.

Use ingredients that you like.

Taste along the way.

Delete, substitute, or add to a recipe to get what you want.

Do it in a controlled way so you know the results of your changes. What I mean is, don't try to do too many changes at once. It takes a little extra time, but it's worth it.

As an example, let's say you think the sauce is too thick, needs more bacon flavor and a little more salt. Don't just add more vinegar, bacon, and salt, and then hope you get lucky.

Do one thing at a time.
Taste after each change.

So let's thin it down first. Based on the way it tastes now, should you add vinegar, apple cider or water? The one you choose, and how much you add, will change the way the sauce tastes.

After the consistency is like you want it, taste again. It may still need something, but now it might be something different.

If you think it still needs bacon and salt too, add some bacon first. Once you do that, **taste it again**. Because bacon is salty, it may not need any salt now.

See how it works?

It's usually pretty logical. Guess what... it should be time for another drink. Have fun with it. Here's to getting better.

11

Sugar Free BBQ Sauce

Make your own sugar free BBQ sauce. You know it will be better than what you might be able to find in the stores (if you can even find it at all).

I know things that I show you and talk about almost always seem to have brown sugar or molasses in them. That's because I like at least some sweetness in my BBQ sauce. So does most of my family.

I have a sister-in-law, though, that cannot eat anything with sugar in it. Not only that, she is restricted from eating foods that create sugars, such as corn.

She is not able to eat potatoes or white flour either. Some fruits are OK, like cherries. But others are not, like grapes. It gets pretty complicated. That's why I just ask, or hand her the label so she can tell me if she can eat it or not.

Every time we get together, we always take a close look at our meal plans so we can be fixing things that she is able eat. Sometimes we end up making two batches of something (a regular version, and another sugar free version with all the right foods).

If you subscribe to Original-Q , (which I wish you would) you'll notice in the January issue that I fixed two different batches of meatballs. That was so my sister-in-law would have some that she could eat.

Over Christmas when I grilled those meatballs (yes, grilled), I also made a second sauce too, which was a sugar free BBQ sauce.

In case you missed it, here is what I did for the meatballs (make them big enough so they won't fall through the grill).

1 lb ground beef
2 Tbl onion
1 clove garlic
1/2 tsp celery salt
pepper (your taste)
1 tsp Worcestershire sauce

After rolling them around on the grill and getting some good grill marks, here is the sauce that I used.

1/4 c vinegar
1/2 c ketchup
1 Tbl brown sugar
1 clove crushed garlic
2 Tbls Worcestershire sauce

Heat the sauce. Add the cooked meatballs and simmer for about 30 minutes. Serve hot.

When I made the sugar free BBQ sauce, I simply left out the brown sugar. Well, I also used tomato sauce instead of ketchup (the label said it had sugar in it).

That seems to make an OK sauce, but people who can't eat sugar like a little sweetness too. So, we just added enough Splenda to give it that needed extra.

Making a sugar free BBQ sauce can be done by simply substituting sugar, brown sugar, molasses, honey, etc., with your favorite form of sweetener.

Just taste along the way so you won't get too much. And also be checking other ingredients for sugar content, such as ketchup, or even some tomato sauces.

By using good quality ingredients, and making sugar free

BBQ sauce yourself, it will almost assuredly turn out better that anything you could buy.

Don't be afraid to give it a try. After a few attempts, you will begin trying new things all the time. Just get yourself another drink and try again.

12
Green Tomatillo Sauce

Give this recipe a try. If necessary you can tweak it to your liking.

2 pounds green tomatoes chopped
2 pounds tomatillos, husked and chopped
3 garlic cloves
1 cup brown sugar
1 ½ cup cider vinegar
1 cup diced red onion
1 tablespoon dry mustard
1 teaspoons salt
1 tablespoons Tabasco sauce

Sautee garlic and onion in butter or olive oil until onions are translucent. Add all other ingredients and cook until tomatillos and tomatoes are tender. Take off heat and allow to sauce to reduce temperature. When at room temperature add everything to food processor and blend until smooth.

This is just a little change of pace. It is a good sauce to use on smoked or grilled meats. It's also a good sauce just to have around while you are grilling for dipping tortilla chips.

13
Vinegar Based Barbecue Sauce
We're Not in Kansas Anymore

Let's talk only about vinegar based barbecue sauce. How's that?

You might think that this really narrows down the choice of sauces.

Well... Yes and no.

We have eliminated tomato based sauces, sure, but that still leaves us with everything east of the Mississippi river.

Let's get out of Kansas City and head toward the east coast.

Lots of sauces have a combination of vinegar and tomato as a base. If we cut out everything but the vinegar, that takes us all the way to North Carolina (actually eastern North Carolina).

This is the home of the vinegar based barbecue sauce. Of course its popularity has spread all across the country. So hopefully everyone has had a chance to try it (unless they are so deep into another style that no other is allowed in).

From there, BBQ sauce recipes have less vinegar and more additional ingredients the farther away you travel (all the way to back to Kansas City, where they use very little or no vinegar).

If we tried to create a map of the United States showing

the location of all the styles of BBQ sauce, with all of the regional and local variations, it would look like a 1600s map of Indian tribes with all their associated bands. There would be hundreds of them (maybe more).

Down to the Basics

The most pure form of vinegar based barbecue sauce would be straight vinegar (preferably apple cider vinegar), with maybe a touch of salt and pepper. Quite often it is flavored with some red pepper flakes or a little cayenne pepper.

This helps the meat stay moist, tenderizes it, and flavors it. It's no wonder people keep using it.

1 1/3 C cider vinegar
2/3 C water
1 Tbl salt
1 tsp chili powder

Something like this, or any other form of vinegar based barbecue sauce, should be made a day in advance, if possible. That gives the vinegar time to break down the seasonings and absorb them.

Remember that you control the flavors.

Add your favorite spices, change the type of vinegar, use more or less water... it's entirely up to you.

You can even add things like tomato sauce, ketchup or mustard. Just don't go overboard or you will end up back in Kansas City, with no vinegar, looking for a different article.

Have you ever had pulled pork and wondered how in the world they ever got it to taste that good? Naturally the quality of the meat, and how expertly it was smoked, had something to do with it. But, the finishing touch and the final balance of flavors probably came from a vinegar based barbecue sauce (like this one).

1 c cider vinegar
1/4 c brown sugar
1 tsp crushed red pepper flakes
1 tsp cayenne pepper
1/2 tsp salt
1/2 tsp pepper

Mix all ingredients together and let stand for at least 4 hours for full flavor. If you don't like the stronger flavor of cider vinegar, replace it with white vinegar. Or, maybe, add another cup of white vinegar to the cider vinegar and double everything else.

Here is another form of vinegar based sauce that has a little different spin to it.

1 1/2 c cider vinegar
1 Tbl chili powder
1 Tbl brown sugar
1 1/2 tsp salt
1 tsp black pepper
1 tsp paprika
1 tsp dry mustard
1/2 tsp cumin

Again, with this one, mix it together and let it set for a few hours for flavor infusion. As you know, you can adjust the seasonings and the amounts of either recipe to suit your taste.

Both of these can be used as a mop or basting sauce, as well as the finishing sauce. Actually any basic vinegar sauce can be used as

a **marinade** *(before smoking)*,
a **mop sauce** *(used during smoking)*,
a **finishing sauce** *(applied at the end of smoking)*,
or a **dipping sauce** *(at the table)*.

Unlike tomato based sauces, vinegar based BBQ recipes

are used at all stages of the cooking process.

Tomato based sauces have sugars that can burn. They are normally used as a finishing sauce and added during the last minutes of smoking. Usually those tomato sauces have a few more ingredients and are also thicker.

Vinegar is powerful stuff.

It is acidic and will penetrate meat. It aids with tenderization and helps to allow the pork to be pulled apart (vinegar based barbecue sauce is most often used with pulled pork).

Because of this characteristic, if the vinegar is flavored, it will also get flavor deep into the meat. By using it early and often during smoking, the flavors will intensify.

This North Carolina type of vinegar based barbecue sauce goes perfect with pulled pork. Please remember, though, you can make these match your own taste by changing, adding or deleting ingredients.

* To make it less spicy, decrease the cayenne or red pepper flakes.

* To make it sweeter, add some honey, molasses, or more brown sugar.

* Thicken it by adding a little ketchup or mustard or molasses.

* Thin it by adding more vinegar, some wine, or a little water.

You know how it works. Work with it in small batches, and get it the way you like it. Record it somewhere so you can duplicate your efforts. So... go get yourself another drink and let's get started.

Thank You

Well, you have arrived at the end of **Your BBQ Sauce is Best**. First, I want to thank you for buying my book. Second, I want to encourage you to never stop learning about BBQ. The more you can learn, the more confident you will become.

Whether you are working on one recipe or dozens, keep working to perfect them (for your own taste). If I have taught you anything with this book, I hope it is to have shown you that, not only do you have the power to make recipes taste the way you want, you also have the ability. All you need is a little good information, experience, and confidence.

It begins to snowball after a while. You start with a little new information. Then you try it out (experience). From the experience, you gain confidence and more information. That boost in confidence and new information makes you want to try again (more experience). And so on...

Thank You.

About the Author

Jeff Slankard is the creator of
http://www.original-bbq-recipes.com/.
A lifelong BBQer trying to spread the good news of BBQ
so others can enjoy the relaxation, leisure, and fellowship
that BBQ can offer.

Other books and/or e-books written
by **Jeff Slankard**
BBQ Basics – Selected Topics for the BBQ Beginner
Beyond BBQ Basics – BBQ Facts, Tips and Techniques
That Come From Experience
Original BBQ Recipes – Create Your Own Unique BBQ,
Tested and Approved by You

Connect with Jeff (Hipshot) online
Website: http://www.original-bbq-recipes.com/
e-zine: http://www.original-bbq-
recipes.com/original_q.html
blog: http://www.original-bbq-recipes.com/bbq-recipes-
blog.html

CPSIA information can be obtained at www.ICGtesting.com
Printed in the USA
LVOW12s1917130614

389983LV00027B/889/P